D1296816

IMAGES
of America

CLEVELAND
METROPARKS

Puritas Springs Road, pictured in the summer of 1920, demonstrates why early park planners were so resolved to preserve the Rocky River valley for future generations. (Cleveland Metroparks.)

On the cover: Shown here in June 1939 are the dam and Albion Road Bridge at Bonnie Park in Strongsville. (Cleveland Press Collection, Cleveland State University.)

IMAGES
of America

CLEVELAND
METROPARKS

Thomas G. Matowitz Jr.

ARCADIA
PUBLISHING

Copyright © 2006 by Thomas G. Matowitz Jr.
ISBN 0-7385-4069-2

Published by Arcadia Publishing
Charleston SC, Chicago IL, Portsmouth NH, San Francisco CA

Printed in the United States of America

Library of Congress Catalog Card Number: 2006924959

For all general information contact Arcadia Publishing at:
Telephone 843-853-2070
Fax 843-853-0044
E-mail sales@arcadiapublishing.com
For customer service and orders:
Toll-Free 1-888-313-2665

Visit us on the Internet at http://www.arcadiapublishing.com

*To my parents, who made certain that their own love of the park
was transferred to me very early in life.*

CONTENTS

ACKNOWLEDGMENTS

This book would not have been possible without the cooperation of the Cleveland Metroparks staff. At the headquarters, Jane Christyson showed immediate cooperation, readily granting permission to use photographs from the park's own extensive collection. Cleveland Metroparks photographer Casey Batule extended himself to guide me through the park's collection of early photographs and went to great lengths to make certain that they were copied in a way that did them justice. Cleveland Metroparks historical interpreter Foster Brown proved an excellent source of information while warmly embracing the project from its beginning.

Once again, I must thank my friends Bill Barrow and Lynn Duchez Bycko at Cleveland State University's Special Collections Department. Several excellent images appear in this book through the courtesy of the Berea Historical Society. Also I appreciate the help of my friend Matt Grabski, who spent many hours carefully scanning photographs. Finally I am grateful to Arcadia Publishing. Through this book, I was given a great opportunity to become reacquainted with an old friend—Cleveland Metroparks.

Thomas G. Matowitz Jr.
Mentor, Ohio
May 15, 2006

INTRODUCTION

It is rare, after the successful completion of a complex task, for one person to merit or receive the bulk of the credit. Local history provides very few examples where this may be justified, but the story of the origins and development of the Cleveland Metropolitan Park District may be a valid one.

More than a century ago, at the age of 27, William A. Stinchcomb proposed in writing the need for a comprehensive system of parks to surround Greater Cleveland. A glance at maps of the area drawn 100 years ago emphasizes Stinchcomb's remarkable vision. At a time when the city's surroundings were rural and undeveloped, he foresaw the day, in his own lifetime, when his proposed park system would become a precious bulwark against urban sprawl.

Today that is the exact purpose the park serves, and several generations of Greater Cleveland residents have reason to be grateful. It is by no means a thing of the past. The park's message still resonates, and generations to come will find that Cleveland Metroparks will provide a lifetime of opportunities to experience conservation, education, and recreation firsthand.

Farms occupied much of the Rocky River Valley before the park came. Roads were built to connect the farmers to nearby towns. This bridge, a type known as a bowstring, carried Cedar Point Road across Rocky River in the early 20th century. Cedar Point is the location at which the east and west branches of Rocky River converge. (Berea Historical Society.)

William J. White was a wealthy Great Lakes ship owner in the late 19th century. As an avocation, he raised trotting horses at his Two Minute Stock Farm in the Rocky River Valley. The name was taken from the speed of his fastest horse. For many years, the former horse farm has been the site of the Big Met Golf Course. (Cleveland Metroparks.)

One

Before the Park District Existed

At the beginning of the 20th century, Cleveland was one of America's largest cities. Its population was approaching 400,000 and it had a large industrial base. Still it was not necessary to travel very far beyond the city limits to find vast acreage of woods and farmland and a rural agrarian lifestyle little changed since the mid-19th century.

This makes the foresight of William A. Stinchcomb all the more remarkable. Writing in 1905, he stated the following:

> Through the valleys of Rocky River on the west, and the Chagrin River on the east, lie some of the finest stretches of natural park lands to be found in the northern part of Ohio. While all of this is now entirely outside the city, it will be but a short time before they will be inside or very near the limits of 'Greater Cleveland' and it seems to me that they should be secured for the benefit of the entire public before private enterprise or commercial industry places them beyond reach.

While Stinchcomb's idea certainly had merit, it was several years before action was taken to create the park system he envisioned. The first step was taken in 1911, when the Ohio State Senate passed a bill that authorized the creation of park boards and empowered them to receive gifts of land to form parks. Cuyahoga County's newly appointed board of park commissioners met for the first time in March 1912.

In the early 20th century, only two railroad viaducts crossed Rocky River near Bagley Road in Berea. The third was yet to be built. Here a water-powered mill slowly collapses in the left foreground. Seen within the left-hand arch of the nearest bridge, a small business is powered by steam. (Berea Historical Society.)

A swinging bridge provided a perilous path across Baldwin Creek for laborers crossing to the stone quarries in the late 19th century. (Berea Historical Society.)

The Berea quarries were known for their grindstones. The McDermott Company was a large supplier, as demonstrated by the hundreds of finished grindstones stacked in the yard awaiting shipment. The former site of this factory is now occupied by an apartment building. (Berea Historical Society.)

For nearly a century, this area has been marked by three railroad viaducts. The absence of the final one, constructed in 1909, establishes an earlier date for this photograph. Judging by the wooden boxcars with truss rods, it is probably much earlier. Note the brakemen standing on the roof walks, a practice deemed unsafe and stopped many, many years ago. (Berea Historical Society.)

As the inscription on its lower right corner indicates, this stone carving was executed by a local farmer named Henry Church in the year 1885. This is one of the oldest known photographs of Squaw Rock, taken in 1902 by the author's great-grandfather George M. Scott. (Author's collection.)

The Cleveland, Columbus, and Southwestern Railway interurban line once crossed Rocky River on this bridge, shown here under construction. Interurbans were electric railroads that moved people and goods at a lower cost and, some would argue, in greater comfort than the steam-powered competition. They had largely become a thing of the past by the 1930s, and the steel structure of this bridge was probably recycled in a World War II scrap drive. (Berea Historical Society.)

The Berea stone quarries ceased operations so long ago that it is easy to forget how extensive they once were. An age of very relaxed ideas about corporate liability is evidenced by the absence of fences around the property and the presence of spectators, who approached the work site as close as they dared. The houses in the background stood on East Bridge Street. (Berea Historical Society.)

With Rocky River in the background, a man on a high-wheeled bicycle overtakes a barefoot boy on his pony. This view, photographed in Berea around 1895, provides a vivid glimpse of life in the area before Cleveland Metroparks existed. It is obvious why the newly introduced bicycles with wheels of equal size quickly became known as "safety" bicycles. (Berea Historical Society.)

The bridge under construction in the distance was built to carry Bagley Road across Rocky River. The deck plate girder bridge in the foreground served the short line railroad operated by the Cleveland Stone Company to support its quarry operations. (Berea Historical Society.)

Construction of the Bagley Road Bridge is nearly complete in this early-20th-century photograph. The foundation of an abandoned structure deteriorates in the foreground. Note the remaining scaffold and the observers on the bridge deck. (Berea Historical Society.)

Stone quarries presented a treacherous work environment. The worker in the foreground, operating a power tool to cut stone, is surrounded by posts, derricks, a railroad, and unsecured blocks of sandstone. (Berea Historical Society.)

Increasing traffic called for a third railroad bridge across Rocky River in 1909. This odd structure is the partially completed wooden form used to build the new bridge. Unlike its neighbors, which were made of stone blocks, the new span was composed of poured concrete. It remains in use today. (Berea Historical Society.)

Long occupied by a farm family in the Rocky River Valley, this house is now part of the Frostville Museum, a function of the Olmsted Falls Historical Society. From time to time, it is open to the public so visitors can see a glimpse of life in the valley before the coming of the park. (Photograph by the author.)

This forest glade, pictured in 1924, plainly shows the type of land the park district preserved unspoiled for future generations. (Cleveland Metroparks.)

Two

THE CREATION
OF THE PARK DISTRICT

The movement to create the park district began to gather momentum. By 1915, William A. Stinchcomb was serving, without salary, as the park board's engineer. At the same time, he was in touch with Frederick Law Olmsted, seeking his services as a consulting engineer and landscape architect.

Olmsted learned his profession from a master, his own father, one of the greatest landscape architects this country has ever produced. The younger Olmsted was a renowned landscape architect himself, and at Stinchcomb's request, he made two trips to Cleveland in 1915 to inspect the land the park hoped to acquire. He strongly endorsed the plans for the proposed park.

The timing was good. Improving roads and the increased availability of inexpensive cars for the masses made the concept of parks connected by boulevards seem more practical and desirable than would have been the case 10 years earlier.

Various legal challenges remained to be overcome, but a new law creating a park board with real power was passed in March 1917. The new board held its first meeting on July 30, 1917. In 1920, the law authorizing the park was modified to include a provision to seek funding through tax levies. In 1921, William A. Stinchcomb became the first director of the Cleveland Metropolitan Park District.

Taken in 1920, this view shows a portion of the Rocky River Valley. Cedar Point, nearly empty of trees, is in the distance, and farms and fields under cultivation dominate the foreground. The farms and fields are long gone and a thick forest of pines has covered Cedar Point for decades. (Cleveland Metroparks.)

Some 80 years later, this is how the same area looks today. The house surrounded by trees in the middle distance may be seen in the above photograph and also in the top image on page 16. (Photograph by the author.)

The crumbling ruin of a long-vanished technology, this structure was once a gristmill owned by the Lawrence family. The scene was photographed in 1925. (Cleveland Metroparks.)

What now remains of the Lawrence mill is located within walking distance of the Rocky River Nature Center. (Photograph by the author.)

Taken in about 1921 in the Rocky River Reservation, this view shows Cedar Point on the left and Rocky River in the foreground. The houses visible in the middle distance are evidence of the many farms once found in the area. (Cleveland Metroparks.)

Known as Fort Hill, this ridge is now heavily forested. A hiking trail protected by a sturdy fence permits visitors a beautiful view of the valley in safety. (Cleveland Metroparks.)

Early in the 20th century, this bridge carried Lewis Road across Rocky River. (Cleveland Metroparks.)

The modern Lewis Road Bridge is seen from the same vantage point about 80 years later. (Photograph by the author.)

Mules seem to be doing most of the work during the construction of Hinckley Dam in the spring of 1927. (Cleveland Metroparks.)

Very much a thing of the past now, steam was the prime mover of American industry during the building of the Hinckley Dam in the late 1920s. Here a donkey boiler provides some of the power necessary to get the job done. (Cleveland Metroparks.)

Works Progress Administration (WPA) workers labor on a road improvement in Big Creek Reservation in June 1938. Unlike Civilian Conservation Corps (CCC) workers, these were local men recruited for service in their own communities. (Cleveland Metroparks.)

Property once owned by the Stadler family became part of Big Creek Reservation, located just south of Snow Road. It is seen here in the summer of 1924. (Cleveland Metroparks.)

The dam forming Hinckley Lake is made primarily of earth, as this view demonstrates. Here, with the gradually filling lake on the right, sightseers enjoy the view from the dam's parapet on July 25, 1927. (Cleveland Metroparks.)

The same scene is depicted here in May 2006, 80 years after the dam's completion. (Photograph by the author.)

The completed dam at Hinckley Lake is pictured in the summer of 1939. (Cleveland Metroparks.).

A similar view of Hinckley Dam was photographed in the spring of 2006. (Photograph by the author.)

A sign advertising boat rentals is visible at Bonnie Park in Strongsville in July 1932. The building and the superstructure of the bridge are long gone, but the stone pier, abutments, and dam still mark the site today. (Cleveland Metroparks.)

Swimmers' heads dot the water in Bonnie Park on a hot summer day in the early 1930s. The bridge carried Albion Road across Rocky River. (Cleveland Press Collection, Cleveland State University.)

This diver demonstrates good form as he leaps from a diving board into Rocky River at Bonnie Park. Now only the stonework remains. (Cleveland Press Collection, Cleveland State University.)

In the summer of 1936, concrete walls were constructed on each bank of Rocky River just above the dam in Bonnie Park. Their purpose was to create a swimming area. (Cleveland Press Collection, Cleveland State University.)

This shelter house, seen shortly after completion, was built by the CCC in Bonnie Park. (Cleveland Press Collection, Cleveland State University.)

These young women prepare for a day of swimming in Rocky River in the summer of 1939. (Cleveland Press Collection, Cleveland State University.)

Surveyors found steady employment throughout the park district during the 1930s. This group paused during work in the summer of 1936. (Cleveland Metroparks.)

Visibly similar to the forest surrounding it, this culvert provides another excellent example of the stonework created throughout the park by the CCC in the 1930s. (Cleveland Metroparks.)

Some surprisingly large trees could be moved and transplanted with equipment available in the 1930s. One such task is underway in Euclid Creek Reservation in 1936. (Cleveland Metroparks.)

Built in Euclid Creek Reservation during the mid-1930s, these structures blended well with the natural environment and were seen throughout the park district. (Cleveland Metroparks.)

Three

THE PARK
DISTRICT MATURES

The size of the park grew dramatically during the 1920s. Beginning with just 109 acres, by the end of the decade the park could claim 9,000 acres distributed across nine separate reservations.

Construction to make this land accessible began on a large scale and included roads, baseball fields, and picnic grounds. Since much of the land in the valleys had been cleared by farmers, an ambitious program of reforestation began. These newly planted trees gradually attained their full growth and helped to restore an ecosystem badly damaged and prone to flooding and erosion.

The 1920s also saw construction of golf courses in Rocky River Reservation and the building of a dam to create Hinckley Lake. The newly created 100-acre lake provided a great venue for fishermen, swimmers, and boaters.

The country's economy was badly damaged by the stock market crash in 1929, but progress for the park continued in the 1930s. New Deal agencies like the WPA and the CCC provided labor to complete many important park projects.

This substantial stone structure replaced the earlier bowstring bridge that had once carried Cedar Point Road across Rocky River. Constructed in the early 1930s, it remains in daily use. (Cleveland Metroparks.)

In the 1920s, these wooden steps aided hikers in climbing to the top of Fort Hill in Rocky River Reservation near Cedar Point Road. (Cleveland Metroparks.)

The steam shovel in the distance and the horse-drawn grader in the foreground were used in the late 1920s. This scene shows a retaining wall and channel-widening project near the Tyler barn in Rocky River Reservation. (Cleveland Metroparks.)

With the middle distance obscured by trees, the same view was photographed in May 2006. (Photograph by the author.)

A team of horses provides the power as laborers work to reconstruct the first green on the golf course known as "Little Met," located in Rocky River Reservation, in October 1931. (Cleveland Metroparks.)

Shown is the proposed location of the yet-to-be-built Brookpark Road Bridge as it appeared in April 1932. (Cleveland Metroparks.)

The proximity of the Cleveland Municipal Airport (now Cleveland Hopkins International Airport) to the Rocky River Valley guaranteed that the park would be affected by aircraft accidents. This crash in March 1930 thoroughly demolished the airplane involved and took the lives of an aircraft salesman and his prospective customer. (Cleveland Press Collection, Cleveland State University.)

Long the focal point of the Manakiki Golf Course, the clubhouse was built as a summer residence for the Hanna family in the early 20th century. It is seen shortly after the property was donated to the park district in this June 1945 photograph. (Cleveland Metroparks.)

Although a fire did serious damage in the early 1960s, the house was carefully refurbished and continues to serve visitors today. (Photograph by the author.)

Well-dressed men place a birdhouse in the North Chagrin Reservation sometime in the 1930s. The leather strap over the shoulder of the man in the light suit may have supported a camera case. Perhaps the group was made up of dedicated birdwatchers. (Cleveland Metroparks.)

Using methods known to the ancient Egyptians—a pulley and an inclined plane—the young man in the foreground moves a stone block into place while helping with the construction of a retaining wall during the 1930s. (Cleveland Metroparks.)

Brecksville's Chippewa Creek is pictured in the summer of 1921. Station Road crossed the arched bridge visible in the background. The stone posts supporting the rock ledge are notable. (Cleveland Press Collection, Cleveland State University.)

This view of a waterfall was taken along Chippewa Creek in Brecksville Reservation more than 80 years ago. (Cleveland Metroparks.)

In addition to stonework, poured concrete was employed in the construction of many bridges in the park in the 1930s. Despite its shaky appearance, when completed, this structure would serve as the form for a bridge to be constructed in South Chagrin Reservation in 1931. (Cleveland Metroparks.)

Upon completion, the bridge displays its beautiful symmetry. (Cleveland Metroparks.)

The road to Squires Castle is shown in 1920. (Cleveland Metroparks.)

Although this photograph was taken in North Chagrin Reservation more than 50 years ago, the scene is repeated across the park district every day. (Cleveland Metroparks.)

Once located in North Chagrin Reservation, this is typical of the signage that greeted visitors during the park's early days. (Cleveland Metroparks.)

Ponds and waterways form a vital link in the park's ecosystem. These water lilies grew in North Chagrin Reservation in June 1931. (Cleveland Metroparks.)

One of Cleveland Metropark's goals has always been to provide children from the city and suburbs with an opportunity to learn about the birds and wild animals that inhabit the forests around them. In September 1931, this young visitor becomes acquainted with Oscar, a tame sparrow hawk. (Cleveland Metroparks.)

A curious combination of construction equipment is illustrated in this photograph taken in the mid-1930s. In the right foreground, a steam-powered winch rests between tasks. In the center, a bulldozer works to prepare a parking lot in Euclid Creek Reservation. The photograph was taken in the mid-1930s. (Cleveland Metroparks.)

Shown here is the parking area of the previous image, as it looked after the artisans finished their work. (Cleveland Press Collection, Cleveland State University.)

Adele von Ohl Parker and her place of business, Parker's Ranch, were an institution in the Rocky River Reservation for over 30 years. Located on Mastick Road, Parker's Ranch introduced hundreds of area residents to the Rocky River Valley every year from 1929 until her death in the 1960s. Parker is seen here in July 1930, shortly after her arrival in Cleveland. (Cleveland Press Collection, Cleveland State University.)

This station wagon from Parker's Ranch gathered neighborhood children and brought them to the ranch for a day of fun in August 1940. (Cleveland Press Collection, Cleveland State University.)

Horses seek relief from summer heat and humidity just like the rest of us. Riders from Parker's Ranch help their horses cool off in Rocky River in August 1940. (Cleveland Press Collection, Cleveland State University.)

In a scene that lingers in the memory of a generation of Greater Clevelanders, Adele von Ohl Parker, mounted on the white horse, leads a group of young riders down the trail from Parker's Ranch and into the Rocky River Valley in May 1940. (Cleveland State University; photograph by Byron Filkins.)

The children who rode at Parker's Ranch sometimes ventured to Cleveland to compete in events. On one such outing, Parker and some of her young friends pose in front of the former home of Sylvester Everett on Euclid Avenue. When this photograph was taken in May 1932, the structure was one of the last remnants of Cleveland's famed Millionaire's Row. (Cleveland Press Collection, Cleveland State University.)

In August 1953, children demonstrate their riding skills at Parker's Ranch, a scene repeated many times over the years. The house and barn across the street were the facilities of Mastick Road Stables. (Cleveland Press Collection, Cleveland State University.)

Known as the Music Mound, this site is located in the Rocky River Reservation near Berea. Here the Baldwin-Wallace College band presents a concert in the summer of 1945. (Cleveland Metroparks.)

The Music Mound continues to serve its intended purpose today. (Photograph by the author.)

The West Branch of Rocky River in Hinckley is pictured before the creation of the Hinckley Lake dam in the late 1920s. (Cleveland Metroparks.)

On a distant summer day more than 80 years in the past, this magnificent beech tree provided shade along the park drive in South Chagrin Reservation. (Cleveland Metroparks.)

Area schools were quick to recognize the educational possibilities the park district presented. Here a summer class from Western Reserve University attends a lecture in July 1936. (Cleveland Metroparks.)

A steam shovel assists a road-grading crew in North Chagrin Reservation during the summer of 1938. (Cleveland Metroparks.)

Some of Euclid Creek Reservation's most distinctive features are its cliffs and rock formations. (Cleveland Press Collection, Cleveland State University.)

The framework of a rustic bridge is seen during construction of a trail in North Chagrin Reservation during the mid-1930s. (Cleveland Metroparks.)

These timbers would soon support the roadway of a bridge in North Chagrin Reservation in the mid-1930s. (Cleveland Metroparks.)

A remnant of activity in the area before the park existed, this stonework was once part of an old mill. (Cleveland Metroparks.)

Swimmers cool off near the Albion Road Bridge at Bonnie Park in Strongsville in July 1935. (Cleveland Metroparks.)

With the swimmers and the bridge itself long departed, the same scene is pictured in May 2006. (Photograph by the author.)

The wading pool in Bonnie Park was already something of a local institution in July 1952. Playing in this pool a decade later is one of the author's earliest childhood memories. (Cleveland Press Collection, Cleveland State University.)

Looking downstream from a point below the Bonnie Park dam in October 1936, this view presents the massive arched bridge that carried Pearl Road across Rocky River. A new bridge replaced it years ago. (Cleveland Press Collection, Cleveland State University.)

These happy boys enjoy an outing at the American Legion Camp in North Chagrin Reservation during the summer of 1939. (Cleveland Metroparks.)

Horseback riding has been an important part of the park district's activities since its beginning. These horses and riders explore a bridle trail in North Chagrin Reservation during the 1940s. (Cleveland Metroparks.)

In the late 1930s, Girl Scouts learn firsthand about a sparrow hawk at the Trailside Museum in North Chagrin Reservation. (Cleveland Metroparks.)

Typical of the new structures being built in the park in the 1930s, this is the shelter house in South Chagrin Reservation as it appeared in May 1936. (Cleveland Metroparks.)

The farms on the valley floor, although gone now, provide a glimpse of what life in the area was like before the coming of the park. Across the valley on the bluffs is Mastick Road. (Cleveland Metroparks.)

The growth of trees on the valley floor makes it difficult to recognize that this is the same view, seen nearly 70 years later in the spring of 2006. (Photograph by the author.)

Pete the raccoon imparts a lesson about outdoor life to a young North Chagrin Reservation visitor in September 1931. (Cleveland Metroparks.)

When the park district was established, for cost reasons many crossings of Rocky River were accomplished by fords. Cars of the day had higher ground clearance, but their drivers took a chance crossing the fords on days like this. (Cleveland Press Collection, Cleveland State University.)

The fords across Rocky River did not become less treacherous with the passage of time, however. The car in the background has ventured too deeply onto a flooded ford. The 1953 Mercury in the foreground struggles to pull the other car to safety before it succumbs to the same fate. (Cleveland Press Collection, Cleveland State University.)

This group of railroad viaducts has been a landmark in Rocky River Reservation near Bagley Road in Berea, for generations. The viaducts were built to carry the east–west mainlines of competing railroads across Rocky River. This photograph was taken around 1920. (Cleveland Metroparks.)

Carrying rolling stock its designers could never have envisioned, the same bridge remains in daily service nearly a century after its completion. (Photograph by the author.)

During the 1930s, pavement began to replace the park district's dirt roads. Here is a section of the parkway between Brecksville and North Royalton as it appeared in the summer of 1939. (Cleveland Metroparks.)

WPA workers pour concrete to surface the deck of a bridge nearing completion in Euclid Creek in the mid-1930s. (Cleveland Metroparks.)

Plain old-fashioned hard work accomplished many of the tasks set for WPA laborers in the 1930s. These men construct a stone wall in Euclid Creek Reservation. (Cleveland Metroparks.)

A temporary sign on the truck advertises an upcoming event to recognize the valuable work done by the CCC. (Cleveland Metroparks.)

The structures in the CCC camps were built to be secure and comfortable and to provide a pleasant environment for off-duty workers. This building was located in the Euclid Creek Reservation in the mid-1930s. (Cleveland Metroparks.)

Squires Castle, pictured from the front in the 1930s, was constructed to serve as the gate lodge of an estate that was never completed. It became park district property in 1925. (Cleveland Metroparks.)

The opposite side of Squires Castle is seen here in 1939. The structure was built in the 1880s by Feargus Squire, an English immigrant who went on to become a wealthy man through his association with Standard Oil. The building stands today in North Chagrin Reservation. (Cleveland Metroparks.)

Many park visitors are not deterred by winter. These Boy Scouts enjoy themselves in North Chagrin Reservation the day after Christmas in 1930. (Cleveland Metroparks.)

The park formed a police force early in its history. Lt. James K. Hoy sits at the wheel of car No. 5 in the summer of 1939. (Cleveland Metroparks.)

Lt. James K. Hoy enjoyed a long career in law enforcement. He served as head of the park police for many years, retiring in 1967. That same year, park policemen became known as rangers. Here Hoy demonstrates an earlier mode of transportation in the summer of 1939. (Cleveland Metroparks.)

Another illustration of the quality of stonework incorporated into so many park structures, the fireplace in the YMCA camp in Hinckley nears completion in August 1940. (Cleveland Metroparks.)

Once seen throughout the park, stoves of this pattern cooked many meals during the park district's early days and remained in active use for decades. (Cleveland Metroparks.)

In a scene that recalls images of the Civil War, Boy Scouts hold a summer camp at the Mastick game field in July 1938. (Cleveland Metroparks.)

A hiker is dwarfed by a rock outcropping along the Chagrin River in 1939. The location is not far from Squaw Rock in South Chagrin Reservation. (Cleveland Press Collection, Cleveland State University.)

Flooded fords could restrict valley parkway traffic even on nice days. Their vulnerability amply justified construction of bridges like the one visible on the left. (Cleveland Metroparks.)

With little rain in evidence, the long-disused ford is under water in the same view taken 40 years later. A new bridge crosses Rocky River on the left. (Photograph by the author.)

This view of the Lorain Avenue Bridge, taken in the spring of 1936, looks upstream at an early truss bridge predating the park's establishment. (Cleveland Press Collection, Cleveland State University.)

In the spring of 1973, distant golfers concentrate on their game as ironworkers put the finishing touches on the superstructure of a new bridge built to replace the early bridge seen in the photograph above. (Cleveland Press Collection, Cleveland State University.)

A typical park boulevard is pictured in the 1920s. (Cleveland Metroparks.)

In several cases, the channel of Rocky River was moved in order to facilitate road building or to minimize flooding. One such project is underway in the late 1920s. (Cleveland Metroparks.)

A steam shovel lends a hand during one of the periodic reconfigurations of the Rocky River channel. Note the volume of coal smoke and the operator in his cab, completely exposed to the elements. (Cleveland Metroparks.)

In August 1937, these canoeists enjoy a beautiful day on Hinckley Lake. (Cleveland Metroparks.)

This northwest view across the newly completed Hinckley Lake was taken in July 1930. (Cleveland Metroparks.)

Churned from the hoofs of many horses, this bridle trail in Rocky River Reservation is shown in the winter of 1950. (Cleveland Press Collection, Cleveland State University.)

Typical of the quality park structures built in the 1930s by the CCC, the shelter house on Strawberry Lane in North Chagrin Reservation appears in July 1941. (Cleveland Metroparks.)

Carefully constructed stone structures were built to last practically forever, such as this bridge at the Snow Road picnic ground seen during the summer of 1938. (Cleveland Metroparks.)

In the days when Huntington Reservation was John Huntington's summer estate, this house was its centerpiece. Built in the late 19th century, it was destroyed by fire in the 1920s. (Cleveland Metroparks.)

This view was taken near Huntington Beach in the early 1920s. (Cleveland Metroparks.)

Looking to the south, this view shows Porter Creek in the early 1920s. (Cleveland Metroparks.)

It may resemble a lighthouse, but this structure on the bluff at Huntington Beach was built to serve as a water tower when the property was John Huntington's summer residence. The photograph was taken in 1939. (Cleveland Press Collection, Cleveland State University.)

Whether fishing, swimming, or simply watching others, these visitors are enjoying themselves at Huntington Beach in the mid-1920s. (Cleveland Metroparks.)

A vast rhododendron blooms beautifully at Huntington Beach on a spring day in the 1930s. (Cleveland Metroparks.)

Seen in September 1935, this shelter house was one of the early improvements made in the development of Huntington Reservation. (Cleveland Metroparks.)

Huntington Reservation was originally the country estate of wealthy Cleveland businessman John Huntington. This barn was built on the property during his heyday and was still in good condition in November 1941. (Cleveland Metroparks.)

In the early 1920s, a steam-powered derrick places stone blocks to create a breakwater at Huntington Beach. (Cleveland Metroparks.)

Three men enjoy a summer day from their vantage point at the water's edge on Huntington Beach. Visible on the horizon is a plume of coal smoke marking the track of a Great Lakes steamer in the early 1920s. (Cleveland Metroparks.)

Huntington Beach is crowded on a hot summer day in 1948. (Cleveland Metroparks.)

Boys from Hawken School come to the Trailside Museum in North Chagrin Reservation to learn more about the woods on a summer day in the 1930s. (Cleveland Metroparks.)

Illustrating how the fords were meant to work, a car easily crosses Rocky River near Detroit Road in August 1937. (Cleveland Metroparks.)

The graceful arched bridge carried Detroit Road across Rocky River, and the steel span carried the tracks of the Lake Shore Electric Railroad. The tall building on the left is the old Westlake Hotel. Of the three structures, it alone remains. (Cleveland Metroparks.)

Riders in what is now Mill Stream Run Reservation pause not far from Pearl Road in Strongsville during the summer of 1939. (Cleveland Metroparks.)

Before the park existed, the Rocky River Valley was dotted with farms. This building was once a granary standing on a farm owned by the Mastick family. (Cleveland Press Collection, Cleveland State University.)

High school students prepare for a day of volunteer activities in the park district in 1958. (Cleveland Metroparks.)

Seen in October 1946, the road climbing Shepard's Hill connects the valley parkway with Mastick Road, located on the edge of Rocky River Reservation. (Cleveland Metroparks.)

This view of Cedar Point Road was taken on a bright summer day more than eight decades ago. (Cleveland Metroparks.)

This waterfall, pictured in September 1922, lies in the Chagrin River just north of Squaw Rock. (Cleveland Metroparks.)

In September 1918, this old mill stood on the banks of the Chagrin River not far from Squaw Rock. (Cleveland Metroparks.)

Taken in September 1918, this view shows waterfalls on the Chagrin River near Squaw Rock in South Chagrin Reservation. (Cleveland Metroparks.)

The large garage and carriage house on the right, photographed in June 1945, were located near the clubhouse at Manakiki Golf Course. (Cleveland Metroparks.)

This view, taken in March 1964, shows the ruins of an old mill situated on Tinker's Creek in Bedford Reservation. (Cleveland Metroparks.)

Taken in late November 1930,
this view depicts a waterfall on
the Chagrin River in South
Chagrin Reservation.
(Cleveland Metroparks.)

Rather primitive dirt roads like this one served early visitors to South Chagrin Reservation in
the mid-1920s. (Cleveland Metroparks.)

The Chagrin River near Gates Mills is
pictured here in May 1918.
(Cleveland Metroparks.)

Taken in 1920, this photograph shows the route of a proposed drive through South Chagrin
Reservation. (Cleveland Metroparks.)

In the autumn of 1940, this view was taken looking north from the Brookpark Road Bridge. (Cleveland Press Collection, Cleveland State University.)

This early truss bridge was still carrying Royalton Road traffic across Rocky River in 1938. (Cleveland Metroparks.)

A couple walks a deserted park boulevard in Rocky River Reservation in the early spring of 1939. (Cleveland Press Collection, Cleveland State University.)

Taken in August 1937, this view shows the newly completed bridge at Cedar Point. The bridge remains in daily use, 70 years later. The ridgeline above is now covered with tall trees. (Cleveland Metroparks.)

This is the Buttermilk Falls Bridge, situated on Strawberry Lane in North Chagrin Reservation, as it appeared in the early spring of 1939. (Cleveland Press Collection, Cleveland State University.)

Here is the same view, 66 years later. This is quite possibly the last photograph ever taken of the bridge, as it was destroyed the following day to make way for a modern replacement. (Photograph by the author.)

The entire Buttermilk Falls Bridge is seen on its last day in April 2006. (Photograph by the author.)

The newly completed Baldwin Creek Bridge in Berea is pictured in June 1938. (Cleveland Metroparks.)

Evidence of the park's reforestation project, trees surround the Baldwin Creek Bridge in May 2006. (Photograph by the author.)

In 1959, this sycamore near Cedar Point was designated a Moses Cleveland Tree, as it was believed to have been alive when Moses Cleveland arrived in 1796. (Cleveland Press Collection, Cleveland State University.)

The shelter house at Whipps Ledges near Hinckley was photographed in August 1941, shortly after completion. (Cleveland Metroparks.)

This striking photograph, taken in August 1937, emphasizes the park district's progress in its first 20 years—from an idea to a parkway accessible to all. (Cleveland Metroparks.)

This bridge illustrates the excellent quality of work done by the WPA in Euclid Creek Reservation in the mid-1930s. (Cleveland Press Collection, Cleveland State University.)

This retaining wall was constructed in Euclid Creek Reservation in the 1930s. Built by the CCC, it protected a trail from erosion and flooding. (Cleveland Metroparks.)

Taken in July 1948, this view shows part of the timber trestle that once carried the Baltimore and Ohio Railroad across Eastland Road and Rocky River. The structure still exists, buried in fill dirt excavated during construction of the Ohio Turnpike in the early 1950s. (Cleveland Metroparks.)

Rocky River Reservation's YMCA camp building is pictured in the summer of 1939. (Cleveland Metroparks.)

The primitive appearance of this cement truck dates this construction photograph to the late 1920s. It seems hard to believe that a truck like this could deliver its load with any degree of precision. (Cleveland Metroparks.)

WPA laborers are busy with another project to realign the channel of Rocky River in September 1940. The work site was located near Royalton Road in Strongsville. (Cleveland Metroparks.)

Typical of the beautiful scenery to be found in South Chagrin Reservation is the main picnic ground, seen in October 1930. Today this area is known as Sulphur Springs picnic area. (Cleveland Metroparks.)

Cleveland Metroparks offered the first public golf courses available on the west side. Their plus fours and hats place these golfers among the first to enjoy the facilities in the mid-1920s. (Cleveland Metroparks.)

Many groups and clubs established activities in the park. Taken in the spring of 1940, this view shows the Campfire Girls cabin near Abram Creek in Rocky River Reservation. (Cleveland Metroparks.)

On a bleak winter day in the 1930s, a photographer captured one of the bridges constructed in Euclid Creek Reservation by the CCC. (Cleveland Metroparks.)

The CCC was staffed by young men who otherwise could not have found a place in the work force because of the Great Depression. They traveled far from home and lived in camps like this one, located in Euclid Creek Reservation in the mid-1930s. (Cleveland Metroparks.)

Horses and riders have been a constant in the park from the beginning. This foursome was photographed in the late 1950s. (Cleveland Press Collection, Cleveland State University.)

The memorial to William Stinchcomb is located in Rocky River Reservation, close to the first plot of land sold to the park in 1919. The monument is seen here shortly after its completion in November 1958. (Cleveland Press Collection, Cleveland State University.)

Fishing in Rocky River is another great constant in the park's history. These young anglers try their luck in 1958. (Cleveland Press Collection, Cleveland State University.)

Several stables along the Rocky River Valley provided horses to those who wished to make use of the extensive network of bridle trails. In this August 1937 view, the Lorain Road Bridge appears in the distance. (Cleveland Metroparks.)

The picnic area at Snow Road in Big Creek Reservation is pictured in the summer of 1939. (Cleveland Metroparks.)

Very different from the carefully groomed picnic grounds that greet visitors today, this photograph shows the typical conditions seen 80 years ago. (Cleveland Metroparks.)

The park district began as a desire to preserve the Rocky River Valley, motivated by scenes like this. (Cleveland Metroparks.)

Four

A CONTEMPORARY VIEW
OF THE PARK DISTRICT

The park continues the strong pattern of growth established many years ago and maintains a place in the hearts of countless area families. Research for this book involved visits to different park district sites and revealed the constant presence of visitors enjoying themselves. Cleveland Metroparks will soon begin its second century of service, its popularity and value to Greater Cleveland residents unabated.

As the park enters the 21st century, some relics of its distant past remain. Easily seen from a hiking path just south of Baldwin Lake in Berea are the remnants of the Cleveland, Columbus, and Southwestern bridge shown on page 12. (Photograph by the author.)

This evocative photograph was taken in what is now Mill Stream Run Reservation in Strongsville in September 1975. (Cleveland Press Collection, Cleveland State University.)

Off-duty Cleveland Metroparks ranger mounts relax in their well-kept stable in Hinckley in the summer of 1988. (Cleveland Metroparks.)

A park ranger poses with her mount near the Hinckley stables in the summer of 1988. (Cleveland Metroparks.)

In December 1973, young women enjoy tobogganing at the chalet in Mill Stream Run Reservation in Strongsville. (Cleveland Press Collection, Cleveland State University.)

The chalet itself was a newly completed structure in the early 1970s. (Cleveland Press Collection, Cleveland State University.)

Although they are too early to use it, this father and child anticipate completion of a new all-purpose trail in Rocky River Reservation in the spring of 1973. (Cleveland Press Collection, Cleveland State University.)

This timeless photograph shows Strawberry Pond in North Chagrin Reservation in the early fall of 1973. (Cleveland Press Collection, Cleveland State University.)

Golfers concentrate on their game at Sleepy Hollow Golf Course in Brecksville Reservation during the 1980s. This building was replaced by a new structure in 1991. (Cleveland Metroparks.)

To illustrate the changes that have taken place, this photograph shows an active dredge on Baldwin Lake in Berea. The scene cannot be duplicated today since much of the former lake is gone, given over to silt, marsh grasses, and young trees as it is slowly reclaimed by nature. (Cleveland Metroparks.)

The gorge at Chippewa Creek in Brecksville Reservation is pictured in May 2006. (Photograph by the author.)

This typical Mill Stream Run Reservation scene was photographed on the East Branch of Rocky River, approximately three-quarters of a mile south of Baldwin Lake in Berea. (Photograph by the author.)

This waterfall may be seen just north of the railroad viaducts near Bagley Road in Berea. (Photograph by the author.)

Located in South Chagrin Reservation, this is Squaw Rock as it appears today, compare with the century old image on page 12. (Photograph by the author.)

The woods still beckon. Although this photograph was taken in 1939, the timeless appeal of the hiking trail remains one of the park district's most popular attractions. (Cleveland Metroparks.)

Across America, People are Discovering Something Wonderful. Their Heritage.

Arcadia Publishing is the leading local history publisher in the United States. With more than 3,000 titles in print and hundreds of new titles released every year, Arcadia has extensive specialized experience chronicling the history of communities and celebrating America's hidden stories, bringing to life the people, places, and events from the past. To discover the history of other communities across the nation, please visit:

www.arcadiapublishing.com

Customized search tools allow you to find regional history books about the town where you grew up, the cities where your friends and family live, the town where your parents met, or even that retirement spot you've been dreaming about.

MAP SEARCH